# HOT COAL WALKING, HOOPING, AND OTHER MYSTIFYING

# CIRCUS

# SCIENCE

by Alicia Z. Klepeis

Consultant:
Vesal Dini, PhD in Physics
Postdoctoral Scholar at
Tufts University
Center for Engineering Education Outreach
Medford, Massachusetts

CAPSTONE PRESS
a capstone imprint

Edge Books are published by Capstone Press,
1710 Roe Crest Drive, North Mankato, Minnesota 56003
www.mycapstone.com

**Library of Congress Cataloging-in-Publication Data**
Names: Klepeis, Alicia, 1971- author.
Title: Hot coal walking, hooping, and other mystifying circus science / by
   Alicia Z. Klepeis.
Description: North Mankato, Minnesota : Capstone Press, a Capstone imprint,
   [2017] | Series: Edge books. Circus science | Includes bibliographical references
   and index. | Audience: 4 to 6.
Identifiers: LCCN 2017012633 |
ISBN 9781515772811 (library binding)
ISBN 9781515772859 (eBook PDF)
Subjects: LCSH: Circus performers—Juvenile literature. | Circus—Juvenile literature.
Classification: LCC GV1817 .K54 2017 | DDC 791.3—dc23
LC record available at https://lccn.loc.gov/2017012633

**Editorial Credits**
Abby Colich, editor; Heidi Thompson, designer;
Kelly Garvin, media researcher; Laura Manthe, production specialist

**Photo Credits**
Alamy: blickwinkel/fotototo, 19, dpa picture alliance archive, 14, Kevin Britland, 6,
REUTERS, 23, Vova Pomotzeff, 25, Zuma Press, Inc, 21; Getty Images: John Eder, 10-11,
Taxi/Mike Owen, 17, Victor Chavez, 8; Newscom: Andrew Schwartz/Splash News, 26-27,
Georg Wendt/dpa/picture-alliance, 29, UPI/Bertrand Guay/Big Apple Circus, 12, Shutterstock: Jose Gill, 5; Superstock/Hans Blossey/imagebro/imageBROKER, cover

Artistic elements: Shutterstock: 21, benchart, Gun2becontinued, Igor Vitkovskiy, mikser45, Milissa4like, Nimaxs, Roberto Castillo, s_maria, Supphachai Salaeman

Printed In the United States of America.
010364F17

# TABLE OF CONTENTS

# WELCOME TO THE CIRCUS!

Step right up, and prepare to enter the big top. The acts at this circus will mystify you. You'll see acts of all kinds. Jugglers throwing pins into the air. Clowns walking on giant stilts. Unicyclers riding in circles.

From hot coal walking to hula hooping, the circus is full of many mystical acts. Sometimes these stunts look impossible, even magical. But did you know you can see tons of cool science concepts at work in each circus act? Learn some of the secrets — and science — behind the big top's most mystifying stunts.

# DO NOT TRY THIS AT HOME

Circus acts are a blast to watch, but DO NOT try them yourself. Performers spend years training. They practice every day. Performing a circus act without the proper training and correct safety precautions could result in serious injury. Instead, simple activities that you CAN TRY are included in these pages. They will help you understand the science behind the circus. They are safe, easy, and fun!

## CIRCUS FACT

John Bill Ricketts opened America's first circus in Philadelphia in 1793. It had just one ring, or performance area. President George Washington was one of the attendees.

# BED OF NAILS

You eagerly await the first circus act of the night. Soon a man approaches a bed of long, metal nails. The gleaming points of the nails stick straight up. Wearing only shorts, the man carefully lies down on the bed. He has nothing to protect his skin from the 1,000 sharp points. The crowd gasps, but the performer's face shows no sign of pain. Moments later, he slowly stands up. Not a single puncture wound marks his back.

How can someone lie down on a bed of nails without becoming a human pincushion? You might think that the more nails, the more painful this act is. In fact, the opposite is true. When the performer lies on the bed, his weight is more or less evenly distributed across each nail's surface. This means the **pressure** exerted by each nail in a group is much less than if it were a single nail by itself. If the bed has 1,000 nails, the pressure on the performer is spread out onto each nail. So he only feels 1/1,000 of the pressure of a single nail in each spot a nail touches him. That's not enough pressure to puncture his skin or cause much pain.

**pressure**—a force exerted on an object over a particular amount of its surface

# DON'T
## TRY THIS AT HOME

## TRY THIS INSTEAD

Experience how pressure can be divided evenly for yourself. For this experiment, you'll need two one-dozen cartons of eggs and a plastic garbage bag. Spread the garbage bag on the floor. Make sure the eggs don't have any cracks or fractures. Then make sure all of the eggs are set up in the same direction, such as pointy side down. Have an adult or friend help you step onto the first carton of eggs with one foot. Try to make your foot as flat as possible. That lets you spread your weight evenly over the eggs. Slowly shift all your weight onto that leg. Then position your second foot on top of the other carton of eggs. Slowly step off one foot at a time. Did the eggs crack?

# JUGGLING

The first act of the circus left you on the edge of your seat, but there's so much more. A clown walks into the ring. He's holding an armful of juggling pins. He tosses one in the air, then two, then three. He keeps them low, at first. Soon he begins throwing the pins higher in the air. He adds a fourth pin, then a fifth. The crowd cheers.

What makes juggling possible? **Gravity**! If it weren't for gravity, juggling wouldn't exist. Jugglers must work to keep objects aloft while gravity brings them back down, down, down. When a juggler throws an object in the air, he exerts a **force** on the object. That force is stronger than gravity. The pin **accelerates** upward.

The juggler adjusts the force of his throws depending on how much time he needs the pin to stay in the air. The pin's **mass** also affects how much force the juggler must exert. The more mass an object has, the more force he must use to throw it.

gravity—an attractive force that exists between any two objects, including between Earth and everything on it

force—an interaction, such as a push or pull, that changes the motion of an object

accelerate—a change in the motion of an object

mass—a measure of the amount of matter in an object

# DON'T TRY THIS AT HOME

## TRY THIS INSTEAD

It takes lots of practice to juggle three or more objects. Start simple. Begin by throwing one ball up and catching it in the same hand. Adjust the amount of force you use to throw the ball until it reaches eye level. See gravity at work as the ball falls back down. Once you feel comfortable with that skill, try adding a second ball to the mix. When the first ball reaches its highest point, toss the second ball into the air and then catch the first. See how long you can keep both balls in motion.

## CIRCUS FACT

The world record for the number of balls juggled successfully at once is 11. The juggler made 23 catches in a row.

# HOT COAL WALKING

A long row of glowing, orange coals is spread across the ring. You can hear the smoldering coals crackling. Then a man steps into the ring. He's barefoot! He begins to walk across the hot coals. He does not run. He takes one steady step at a time. When he reaches the end of the coals, he steps off and lifts his feet to show the audience. No blisters. No burns on either foot.

Does this hot coal walker have incredibly tough feet? Probably not more than the average person. So how does he do it? A few factors allow someone to walk across hot coals without burns. The coals are pieces of wood. Wood is a poor **conductor** of heat. So are human feet. **Conduction** is how heat is transferred from one thing (the coals) to another (one's feet) by direct contact. If the performer walks at the right pace across the coals, there isn't much time for heat to flow. The coals also must be at the right temperature. When the conditions are just right, his feet don't get burned.

Also, the coals are typically patted down into a flat surface. This allows the coal walker to spread his feet evenly across the surface, preventing the hot embers from being too concentrated in any one spot on his foot.

conductor—a material that lets heat, electricity, or sound travel easily through it
conduction—the transfer of heat through solid material

## CIRCUS FACT

Wood from different types of trees burns
at different temperatures. Olive and locust
wood are too hot for coal walking. Maple and
cherry burn between 900 and 1,000 degrees
Fahrenheit (482 and 538 degrees Celsius).
They work well for coal walking.

# HULA HOOPING

A performer walks into the center ring with several hula hoops. She steps into one hoop and swivels her hips — fast. The shiny hoop moves quickly. It's like a blur. She puts hoops on both arms and starts spinning them. The hoops glide up and down her body and arms. They seem to defy gravity as they quickly swirl. Before long, she has a dozen hoops in constant motion.

How does this performer keep all her hoops spinning? When hula hoops spin, a combination of forces is at work. The person inside the hoops moves her body to propel them around her. In doing this, she exerts an upward force from her hips, arms, or legs. She exerts a turning force, called a **torque**. Torque causes the hula hoops to **rotate** or spin. The hooper needs to spin her body fast enough, applying enough force, to keep the hula hoops moving. If the hooper slows down, the hoops slow and fall to the ground.

# DON'T TRY THIS AT HOME

# TRY THIS INSTEAD

You don't need a hula hoop to see torque in action. Try spinning a roll of packing tape around a broom handle. Can you move the roll of tape up and down the handle while keeping the tape roll spinning? You can also try spinning a ring from your finger around a pen or pencil.

## CIRCUS FACT

The record for marathon hula hooping by one person using a single hoop is 74 hours and 54 minutes straight.

torque—the tendency of a force to rotate an object about an axis
rotate—to turn in a circle

# DIABOLO

"What's next?" you wonder as a young performer enters the ring. He holds what looks like two bowls stuck together. He sets the object, called a diabolo, on a string. A stick is tied to each end of the string. The performer pulls the sticks quickly back and forth. That gets the diabolo spinning on the string. In seconds, the diabolo is moving fast. It climbs up the string, seeming to defy gravity. The performer tosses it high in the air, catching it back on the string. The diabolo spins and hops in an amazing "dance."

How does the diabolo work? When the performer pulls the stick, the string exerts a force on the diabolo's **axis**. The force causes the diabolo to rotate around its axis and gain **angular momentum** — an amount of angular "oomph." As the performer repeats this action, the diabolo rotates faster and faster. Once it's spinning fast enough, it has enough angular momentum for the performer to do tricks like a giant, fancy yo-yo. The amount of angular momentum, or angular "oomph," can be controlled by applying a torque or twisting force to slow down or speed up the rotation.

# DON'T
## TRY THIS AT HOME

## TRY THIS INSTEAD

Spin a top to see angular momentum at work. Spin the top with more force each time. Does it spin faster and for a longer amount of time? How long can you keep its angular momentum going?

**axis**—a straight line around which an object rotates
**angular momentum**—a measure of an object's rotation, involving mass, shape, and speed

# UNICYCLING

A circus performer approaches the ring, carrying his unicycle. He puts the wheel to the ground. Then he carefully sits on the cycle's seat. He wobbles unsteadily, at first. It looks like he may fall forward . . . or maybe backward. Using his feet, he rocks the wheel back and forth. This steadies him. Riding around the arena, he spins and twirls.

Do you know how to ride a bike? You must balance from side to side, or else you'll fall. A unicycler must balance both side to side and front to back. He must keep the wheel under his **center of gravity**. The center of gravity is the point around which the weight of an object is evenly distributed. Gravity can be considered to pull down on the weight of the entire object at that point. Once seated, the rider is working to keep the wheel under his center of gravity before gravity pulls him down.

## CIRCUS FACT

Some unicyclers can juggle while riding. Some do acrobatics.

center of gravity—the point in an object around which its weight is evenly distributed

# ROLA BOLA

A board sits atop a cylinder. The board looks like a skateboard without wheels. You wonder what this circus act could be. Suddenly, a performer jumps onto the board. His body sways to and fro as he tries to gain his balance. The cylinder rolls beneath him. With his arms spread wide, he moves with the cylinder, staying atop the rola bola. Then he pulls balls out of his pocket and begins to juggle. The crowd ooh's and ahh's.

What's the secret science behind the rola bola? In order to stay on the board, the performer must keep the cylinder under his center of gravity. Remember that the center of gravity is where we can consider the force of gravity to be acting on an object, pulling it down according to its weight. When the performer moves from side to side, his center of gravity moves with him. He needs to exert forces on the board so that the cylinder underneath moves to support him under his center of gravity.

# STILT WALKING

Music begins to play as several clowns walk out onto the stage. Wait a minute. These clowns are very tall. They are all wearing stilts. They look like giants. Some stand 9 feet (2.7 meters) tall with their stilts on. They juggle and perform other circus acts as they tower high. With slow, even, steady strides, these super-tall jesters rule the ring.

How come stilt walkers don't fall? Clowns on stilts adapt the way that they walk. With their legs made longer, they have more weight. Their center of gravity has changed. They must keep their center of gravity balanced over the stilts so that they do not tip over. Stilt walkers' legs feel heavier. Their muscles must work harder to move around. They walk more slowly. They end up taking longer steps because where the stilts touch the ground is farther from the pivot point (the walker's hips), as compared to where the bottom of their feet would be without stilts.

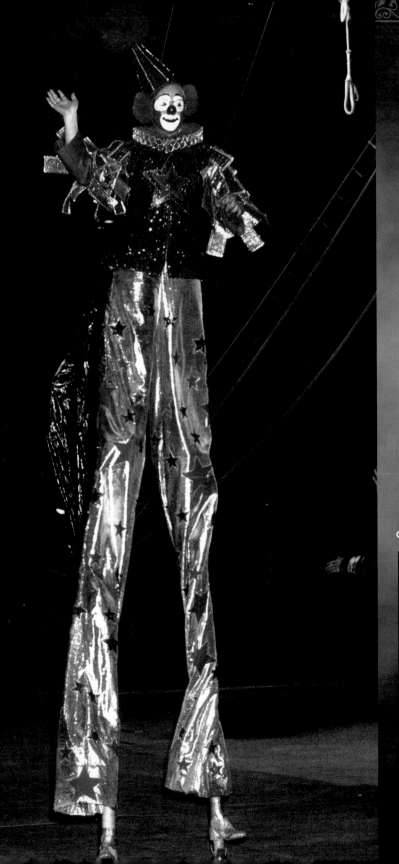

# DON'T

TRY THIS
AT HOME

## TRY THIS
INSTEAD

Try this experiment to test the
balancing ability of stilts. Take
two paper towel or toilet paper
rolls. Place the rolls upright,
about 5 inches (13 centimeters)
apart. Carefully, one at a time,
add books to the top of the
rolls. Make sure the first book's
center of gravity is balanced
evenly over the cardboard
rolls. How many books can
you balance on top of the rolls
before they fall?

## CIRCUS FACT

Stilts aren't just for
circus clowns. Agricultural
workers wear them to
pick fruit and prune trees.
Construction workers wear
them to reach high spaces.
Shepherds use them to look
over their flocks.

# PLATE
# SPINNING

The next **act** involves a plate and a stick. Not very interesting, right? Wrong! A circus performer sets the plate atop the stick. Then she begins rotating the stick between her hands. The plate begins to spin. Then it moves faster and faster. Soon the plate is horizontal. It stays directly above the stick as it quickly spins. Then the performer grabs more sticks and more plates. The plates spin so fast. It's amazing.

What scientific ideas can help us understand plate spinning? A lot of them! As the performer begins to spin the stick, she is applying a torque. **Friction** is the force that keeps the plate from flying off the stick. Once the plate is spinning fast, it has a lot of angular momentum going too, which builds as she applies the torque. The performer also keeps the stick at the center of the plate. That way the plate's center of gravity stays directly above the stick. If the performer stops moving her hands, gravity takes over and the plate falls.

**friction**—a force that opposes the relative motion of two or more surfaces in contact

# GLOBE WALKING

The circus isn't over yet! On the ground you see a large ball. It's about as tall as a school desk. A circus artist climbs onto the ball, waving her arms to gain balance. She shuffles her feet, and the ball quickly starts rolling. The performer moves the ball in all directions as she stays balanced on top. The crowd is wowed.

How does the performer keep everything going at once? Once again, she balances by keeping the globe beneath her center of gravity. She must constantly shift her body to do this. If she leans to the left, her legs won't be able to provide the support to counteract gravity, which will then pull her down. She must quickly lean to the right to counter that unbalanced force.

When a performer leans or has extra weight on one side, she creates a torque (or turning force) that acts to rotate the ball out from underneath her. By leaning the other way, she can create a counter-torque, acting to rotate the ball in the opposite way. As such, she is able to control the direction and motion of the globe.

# POGO STICKS

Bounce! Bounce! Bounce! A rider hops into the center ring on his pogo stick. The harder he pushes down on the stick, the higher he bounces. Before long he does flips and spins in the air.

How is science at work in a pogo stick? When a performer gets onto a pogo stick, he puts his feet on the footpads and holds onto the handlebars. Then he jumps. This jumping motion compresses a spring in the pogo stick. The compressed spring now has energy to give back, called **potential energy**. Then pop! As the spring decompresses, it releases this energy. This energy is converted into the energy of motion of the rider, called **kinetic energy**. The rider is propelled upward.

potential energy—the stored energy of an object that is raised, stretched, or squeezed
kinetic energy—the energy of motion

As gravity works on the pogo stick rider, eventually, he falls back onto the pogo stick and compresses the spring again. The rider pops back up into the air, repeating the process.

## CIRCUS FACT

The world record for the most backflips in a row on a pogo stick is 17.

For this experiment, you'll need a large rubber band, a ruler, chalk, and some open space. You also need a partner. Hook the rubber band onto the ruler's edge, pulling it back, then release the band. Make sure your partner is out of your way first. Next have him mark with the chalk where the band landed. Repeat the process four more times, increasing how far you stretch the rubber band each time. What happens to the distance the rubber band travels (kinetic energy) as you stretch the rubber band (potential energy) more and more?

# SAFETY AT THE CIRCUS

Every circus act comes with risk. Some are riskier than others. It's not as dangerous to hula hoop as it is to walk on hot coals. So how do circus performers stay safe?

All circus artists receive professional training to learn the skills needed for their complicated acts. Around the world there are schools that train people in acrobatics, dance, and theater techniques to prepare them for a future circus career. And there are also certified programs to train circus arts teachers.

Rehearsal is one of the most important preparations for a circus performer. The more times one practices an act such as rola bola, the more skilled he or she gets. The more practice he or she has, the safer it is for him or her to perform in front of an audience.

It's also essential to prepare in case something goes wrong. For example, a stilt walker learns what to do if a stilt breaks or if he or she is about to lose his or her balance and fall. (It happens!) Learning to land in ways that lessen the risk of injury is an important safety skill for many circus performers — from globe walkers to pogo stickers.

# GLOSSARY

**accelerate** (ak-SEL-uh-rayt)—a change in the motion of an object

**angular momentum** (ANG-gyu-lur mom-MEN-tuhm)—a measure of an object's rotation, involving mass, shape, and speed

**axis** (AK-sis)—a straight line around which an object rotates

**center of gravity** (SEN-tur UHV GRAV-uh-tee)—the point in an object around which its weight is evenly distributed

**conduction** (kuhn-DUHK-shun)—the transfer of heat through solid material

**conductor** (kuhn-DUHK-tuhr)—a material that lets heat, electricity, or sound travel easily through it

**force** (FORS)—an interaction, such as a push or pull, that changes the motion of an object

**friction** (FRIK-shuhn)—a force that opposes the relative motion of two or more surfaces in contact

**gravity** (GRAV-uh-tee)—an attractive force that exists between any two objects, including between Earth and everything on it

**kinetic energy** (ki-NET-ik EN-ur-jee)—the energy of motion

**mass** (MASS)—a measure of the amount of matter in an object

**potential energy** (puh-TEN-shuhl EN-ur-jee)—the stored energy of an object that is raised, stretched, or squeezed

**pressure** (PRESH-ur)—a force exerted on an object over a particular amount of its surface

**rotate** (ROH-tate)—to turn in a circle

**torque** (TORK)—the tendency of a force to rotate an object about an axis

# READ MORE

**Doudna, Kelly.** *The Kid's Book of Simple, Everyday Science.* Minneapolis: Scarletta, 2013.

**Gogerly, Liz.** *Circuses.* Explore! London: Wayland, 2017.

**Mercer, Bobby.** *Junk Drawer Physics: 50 Awesome Experiments that Don't Cost a Thing.* Junk Drawer Science. Chicago: Chicago Review Press, 2014.

**Royston, Angela.** *Forces and Motion.* Essential Physical Science. Chicago: Heinemann Library, 2014.

**Turnbull, Stephanie.** *Circus Skills.* Super Skills. Mankato, Minn.: Smart Apple Media, 2013.

# INTERNET SITES

Use FactHound to find Internet sites related to this book.

Visit *www.facthound.com*

Just type in 9781515772811 and go.

# INDEX